Back to Life

How I Overcame the
Obstacles of Christian Dating

Stephanie Genwright

Back to Life

How I Overcame the Obstacles of Christian Dating

Stephanie Genwright

Pure Thoughts Publishing, LLC

BACK TO LIFE

Copyright

solitary and utter responsibility of the recipient reader. Under no circumstances will any legal responsibility or blame be held against the publisher for any reparation, damages, or monetary loss due to the information herein, either directly or indirectly.

Respective authors own all copyrights not held by the publisher.

The trademarks that are used are without any consent, and the publication of the trademark is without permission or backing by the trademark owner. All trademarks and brands within this book are for clarifying purposes only, and are owned by the owners themselves, who are not affiliated with this document. All Rights Reserved.

ISBN: **978-1943409181**

BACK TO LIFE

Dedication

This book is dedicated to my family and all my friends that believed in me and my vision. This book is also dedicated to every woman that had to endure the pain and devastation of a misguided and broken relationship with a man that left you empty. This book is to encourage those that are still going through the devastation to let you know there is hope for you and for those of us who overcame continue to live life.

Table of Contents

BACK TO LIFE

ACKNOWLEDGMENTS

First I would like to thank my Heavenly Father for watching over me and guiding my life all these years. I love you Jesus with every fiber of my being.

I want to thank my family for their unconditional and undying love for me.

To my mother and father for their belief in me and their prayers and support.

To my big sister Fonda Clark for giving me a chance (insider) and for her unselfish prayers and support.

To Safe Haven ministries (My first born) for your belief in me and for your love, prayers and support

To all that are in my inner circle you know who you are thanks for your love and support.

To Latonya Powers who prophesied this book to me in its infant stages. It has come to pass.

To my spiritual father Bishop John W. Barber who has gone on to be with the Lord for all the words of wisdom and spiritual impartations.

To every Apostle, Prophet, Pastor, Teacher, Evangelist that has ever spoke over my life I thank you.

BACK TO LIFE

INRODUCTION

This book in no way is about incriminating anyone. But the reason the Lord gave me this endeavor was to let others know of Gods redeeming Grace and my journey and my destination in life. This book was written for the soul intent of bringing healing, deliverance and restoration to those that has gone through or are currently going through a difficult situation.

My prayer is that you find the determination that you need to keep moving forward in the things of God. There is life after devastation. You have purpose and God has a plan for your life. You are not a failure but you are the handy work of God. Marvelous are the works of His Hands.
Be blessed and empowered,
Humbly submitted,
In His Care
Stephanie Genwright

Chapter 1: The Lure

We as women of God or just women in general want a man of influence and a man that can handle his business. We want a man that can pull his weight in society, a man that's a manly man. We also want a man that is sensitive and understanding and a man that has a vision and in pursuit of it.

So many times we as women we see someone who resembles what we envision as our ideal man even though he may be less than the total package we feel like we can help him cause he has "potential". Then we get all excited tell all our girlfriends and we are off to the races.
Well I might as well get real and tell you my story. I'm just a country girl from rural North Carolina. I grew up in a single parent home with my mother, grandmother and sister. I was always chubby and not that popular in school but I had friends who where. We were a family that occasionally went to church, we were Methodist AMEZ. At the age of 10 or 11 I began to sing on the choir at the AME Church down the street with my cousin. That's when I discovered I had a gift to sing. At the age of 13 I was introduced to

BACK TO LIFE

the holiness church I got saved and was on my way with Jesus. At the age of 16 I was called into the ministry and began preaching the Gospel. I was often misunderstood by those who I looked to for help and guidance. I had very few relationships growing up. I had three boyfriends between the ages of 15-23. I really loved them, all where preachers who eventually got married shortly after we broke up. Wow. I had one other boy friend that treated me well but just was not ready for what I was looking for full commitment.

Then one warm September Sunday afternoon in 1995 it happened I met a mysterious yet intriguing young man whom fit the bill of what I thought was the ultimate and suitable fit for me. He was the very epitome of what I envisioned as the perfect man. As a woman of God of course I had my vision of what I wanted my man to be like. I desired for him to be yea tall and a man of God who could preach, sing, play the organ and had a vision to work in the kingdom of God. We met through a mutual friend. While standing outside of the church after he had preached a moving sermon he came over to me and asked for my phone number. Wow of course I eagerly gave him my number and he gave me his number. He stated, "we will stay in touch I will call you." I was so elated and overjoyed I could hardly contain myself. I a chubby country girl finally met someone who was fine and anointed and was interested in me. You see it's dangerous for a young girl who never had a strong father figure to go into the world. It's dangerous because a part of us is always looking for that validation from a male. You are actually ill-prepared for the world of dating and often times very naive. Fathers it so important to be in your little girl's life she needs your influence.

Well my intriguing man did eventually call me and we immediately hit it off. We had a lot in common ministry, music and a passion for the people of God. He and I had a mutual friend that had a community choir in which I was asked to participate. I sang soprano and they were in need so I decided to help them out. That was a mistake. I had to travel hour and half for rehearsal. Once rehearsals began my knight in shining armor became a little distant. Remember

BACK TO LIFE

I was naive. The women on the choir were after him and our mutual friend so this created tension with the females in the choir. By this time he informed me he only wanted to be friends with me. Major hint reader, if a man says he only wants to be friends he is really saying I only want to see you and talk to you when it's convenient for me. It also says that I don't want to commit to you I don't want to be obligated or accountable to you. That's well and good if they don't start sending mixed signals.

Well I made up my mind to go my separate way because I had enough friends. Well about six months went by and I received a card from my knight while he was in Delaware doing some services for his aunt. The card expressed that he wanted to open up communication with me. I didn't respond. Then I began to receive calls from him in which I ignored for a while. Then he began to leave messages where he would sing. That did it I was a sucker for his singing. We begin communicating via phone. Some time went by and he started a church. He asked me to attend the opening but I didn't. He then began to ask me to come and preach for him. I did because I love to proclaim the Gospel. During this time my Pastor was really sick and eventually died. I then was without a pastor. During this time my knight in shining armor asked me to come to some of his services. I did and as time went on he asked me to help him with the church. I remember that day so well he and I were traveling to a Sunday evening service near his home town. I was so proud to be riding with him to be on his arm, and he seemed to be happy with me on his arm so I thought. Later that day on our way from that service he asked me if I would come and help and assist him with the church. I told him that I would have to pray about it because I didn't want to come to the ministry because of the way I felt about him but if I came I wanted it to be the will of God. He said he understood. I did earnestly pray and I felt the release to help the man of God. I was so elated to be able to help and I was eager to help too eager as I look back.

I started in head first I did praise and worship every Sunday. Then the responsibilities came in like a flood. I was so ministry driven. You know how we women are we put our heart, soul, mind,

BACK TO LIFE

body and resources in something that we love, especially if it involves someone we love. I Lived an hour and half away I was at the church at lease 3-4 times a week. I was hooked I had been reeled in yes LURED IN.

Chapter 2: The Lie

I joined the church of my knight in shining armor. I was so involved in ministry. I participated in every aspect of ministry from church administrator, to praise and worship leader to, leader of women's ministry and yes even custodian. I passed out tracks, walked door to door ministering, hung curtains, taught Sunday school, counseled many, and even fried chicken for plate sales and the list goes on. You see I didn't mind because I loved ministry and by this time I had fallen in love with my knight in shining armor. I was always accessible to my know pastor. You see for a period of time I served as his personal assistant and even served as his personal nurse/armor bearer. Whenever he went out to preach I never missed no matter how far I had to drive or how late we got back. Often when he ministered out I was the one that always introduced him and sang prior to him preaching if the choir wasn't there which was more often than not. There were times I drove for him, you see I didn't mind because usually when we got back he and I would go out to eat. That was our time to hang out. I loved that because we often shared our goals and endeavors. You see I was getting to know him and studying him because in my mind I thought he was feeling the same way I felt. People always put us together as a couple and we never changed the way we did things. For a period of time we were always together in various places church, restaurants, concerts, we traveled together in and out of state, I thought I had secured my place in his life as someone special. I made the terrible mistake of assuming. He never told me that this wasn't what he wanted. He always told me enough to keep me hanging on.

I was so consumed with this man. I would pray for him incessantly. That's not a bad thing but in the process I didn't pray much for myself. I wonder was he praying for me the same way hmmm. You see I put down my dreams and aspirations to ensure that his came to pass. To tell the truth looking back I literally lost myself and my identity all in the name of service and love. That was a train wreck waiting to happen. We as women at times think we have to have a man of influence to make us, but before the foundations of the world God had already equipped us with everything we need to fulfill our purpose in Him. Listen women please never lose your identity or dream or aspiration in a man.

Now you may be wondering why did she entitle this chapter, "The Lie?" When a person doesn't share the truth of how he or she really feel about you especially if they know you have very strong feelings for them then they have not been honest. People often use and manipulate your gifts when you are gullible. The bible says that a little leaven leavened the whole lump. A half truth is a whole lie. In other words an impure motive is a dressed up lie to keep the victim entrapped and used like a puppet on a string. In essences the victim is living in a Lie and living The Lie.

Chapter 3: The Addiction, Illusion, and Fantasy

I was reluctant to start this chapter not because I had writers block or didn't have anything to say. I was reluctant because in this chapter I have to be transparent and open about myself. See I am a private person who prides myself on putting the best on the outside and not allowing anyone to see my less than perfect side. I entitled this chapter the addiction, illusion and the fantasy. So someone maybe saying why this title, there are no drugs or hallucinogens or hypnotics involved. Well I titled it this because though there are no drugs involved or hallucinogens or hypnotics there was defiantly an addition and illusion and a fantasy.

Let's take a look at the word addiction. According to Webster the word addiction means, the quality or state of being addicted; esp.:

compulsive need for habit forming drugs. Let's take a look at the word addict, (1) to devote or surrender oneself to something habitually or excessively, (2) to cause a person to become physiologically dependant on a drug. Let take the word drug out and replace it with the word idea or concept. Because we are creatures of habit and persons with ideas and dreams of what we think is the perfect plan for our life, we often try to make that happen the way we want it to happen no matter what sacrifices we have to make. Because we become addicted to an idea, concept or dream we began to have illusions. According to Webster an illusion is (1) a mistaken idea, a misconception a misapprehension, fantasy. (2) A misleading image presented to the vision. An illusion gives a false sense of security because we see what we want to see thus this leads us into a fantasy world where a look or a kind word can be turned into something fragmented and misinterpreted for something that doesn't exist. Fantasy according to Webster means imagination, a product of the imagination and Illusion. First I like to say that it's nothing wrong with having a health imagination. The problem comes in when your imagination is not the will of God thus leaving you open as a prey for Satan. He is the master manipulator. If he can get a hold to your thoughts and twist them he will have you doing whatever he desires, which is to sift you and eat away at your core or the essences of who you are thus aborting the plan of God for your life. Guard your thoughts with the word of God. Romans 12:1-2 (1) I beseech you therefore brethren by the mercies of God that you present your bodies a living sacrifice holy and acceptable which is your reasonable service.(2) And be not conformed to this world but be ye transformed by the renewing of your mind.

Remember the job of Satan is to steal, kill and destroy. I'm telling you this as a warning because he Satan can sometimes get the best of us meaning those of us who have been in Christ for a while. He can get us if we are not consistent in prayer, the word and fellowship with other believers. So this leads us to my journey of misappropriated feelings, images, thoughts and aspirations.

I shared with you earlier in chapter one that I met this person that is thought was the very epitome of what I wanted in a man, especially in a man of God. After we met and I began going to his church and being a monkey wrench just filling in so diligently in all aspects of ministry from being the janitor to being the praise and worship leader you name it I did it whole heartily. One major mistake I made early on was I was so busy doing church work I didn't make enough time for the Lord of the church. One more mistake I probably will be saying that a lot, but I was too accessible. I made myself available when I probably should not have. Side note women and men always take time for God and yourself. If you don't take time for God you will eventually destruct, if you don't take time for yourself you will lose the flavor of who you are. You need that time to refresh and regroup. Listen my grandmother often said if you don't look out for yourself no one else will. People will take and take and take and take from you. You got to say when enough is enough. He would often say, can't no one use you in the house of God because your gifts don't belong to you they are Gods. I agree to a certain point, but you can be abused which is misuse and abnormal use of the gifts of God.

 I was so intrigued and enthused with this man. I use to think of him incessantly all the time. I would have done almost anything for him. I thought he was my knight in shining armor my soul mate my true love. To make matters worse some of my friends were in agreement with this, that he was my husband. I also had prophets and prophetess to prophesy to me that he was indeed my husband. People of God this is dangerous to prophesy these things because you are talking about people lives. If I didn't know God when things changed I would have lost my mind. I read a book by Miles Monroe entitled, Waiting and Dating. There is a section in the book that talks about there is no such thing as soul mates or that perfect special one, but that we are given the power to choose. There are approximately seven billion people on earth. What is the likelihood of you meeting that one perfect person, that's fantasy and it's a myth. God gives us the power to choose but choose according to the kingdom of God standards and not the world standard. (That was a little side note. now on with the story.) Most places we went in ministry I was always the one mistaken for as the 1ST Lady. Oh yes and I dressed the part and acted out the part. I was always the one that introduced him prior to him preaching, I usually sang a solo for prior to him preaching so I definitely appeared to be the one that was his soul mate and wife to be. I gave so much of myself in hopes that he would marry me one day don't get me wrong I loved God and the ministry and they came first but always in the back of my mind I wished and longed to be the one. I almost lost my identity and myself trying to force something that was not meant to be. This man knew I cared and loved him dearly so he took advantage of the opportunity that presented itself. He would always say just enough to keep me plugged into him. He always knew exactly what to say. I helped him establish the ministry and helped run the ministry. I prayed for the ministry, I labored for the ministry, I gave up much for the ministry, time, effort, energy and finances. I was so addicted, so in an illusion, and living in a fantasy I even gave up my dream and vision for his.

BACK TO LIFE

Women and men too never ever lose yourself in another person only lose yourself in God. In Matthew it says if a man loses his life for Christ sake he will find it. If you lose yourself in a man you may never find yourself except for the grace of God. There is hope and there is rehabilitation for this kind of addiction. There is therapy for this kind of illusion and there is a remedy for this kind of fantasizing. Stay tuned.............

Chapter 4: TAKING RESPONSIBILITY

The road to recovery from addiction of any kind is a long winding road that has its highs, lows, and even setbacks. If you are willing and determined then you will take the challenge. There is a lot of work that has to be done during the recovery stages. It's going to take more than the antics of church to get the emotional healing that's needed. It's going to take more than turning around three times or giving someone a high five and repeating what the preacher says. I'm not in any way trying to minimize the church but so many people continue to lead defeated lives because they only rely on church antics to bring them emotional healing. More times than not it takes great effort and determination to go after and get the emotional healing and deliverance that you need. It's during recovery that you will have to be honest with yourself and began to take a close look in the mirror and began to examine your soul, spirit and conscience. You will have to evaluate all of who you are. We as people of prominence and influence have to beware of the trap of being caught up in who we present ourselves as and what we allow people to try to make us into. If we are not careful we can end up with a false sense of being this perfect picture of a super human that really doesn't exist. This will only set you up for a state of confusion in yourself about who you really are. This is a major problem in the body of Christ. Many people don't know who they are or what their real purpose is in life. This kind of thinking often leads to jealousy and division in the church. If I'm busy trying to be someone else then who is being "the me" that God created me to be?

While on the road to recovery you cannot play the victim forever. There comes a point and time where you will have to take full responsibility for all your actions. In my case at first I only blamed the man for deceiving me, using me, manipulating and leading me on. But I came to my senses yes he did do these things to me and by no means am I letting him off the hook for what he done but I had to realize I allowed him to do these things to me. I had to begin unraveling this situation and began asking myself questions like, why did I let him do this to me? Why did I allow myself to be so gullible? Why did I allow myself to be so accessible and always ready available to heed to his lease beckoning call? Why did I give so much of myself to someone who never relinquished his heart to me? Why was I willing to give up every dream and vision for my life for this man who never gave me the love that I deserved? This is the point where you will either dig for the truth about yourself or remain stuck in the same debilitated state of being the victim. I made up mind to dig a little further into why I accepted this type of treatment. As I began to look at myself and the situation I discovered that even though I had been saved for years there was still the residue of my dysfunctional childhood left lingering around. I knew that my mother loved me to the best of her ability and my Grandmother did the best she could because she was dealing with her own demons as well as my mother. I never had a real male figure that was active in my life as a child or at least not anyone to validate me and make me feel safe. As a child growing up my father was not active in my life he would come

BACK TO LIFE

around every now and then but not often. I'm not blaming him either because I'm sure his own father was not there for him so he didn't have any examples of what fatherhood was suppose to look like. I realized that even as a child growing up and often teased about my weight I had an attitude that I was going to attempt to please everyone and they would look past my weight and like me wow was I wrong. So I found myself being a people pleaser even if it caused me pain. So in retrospect I can see how I took all that foolishness for so long because I thought that by pleasing him that it would make him love me for me, also because I had a false sense of who he really was in my mind I had him pictured as the perfect man for me so I was willing to sacrifice it all to me with him. Chaka Khan said, through the fire through to the limit to the wire for a chance to be with you I'll gladly risk it all. Wow. I have to chuckle at myself now for investing so much into something that gave so little return.

Thank God for looking out for me because I could have lost my mind many people do not recover from situations like this. As I continued to look for the answers and discover who I really was I began to find myself again it was the beginning of my recovery. If you are looking for emotional healing you must take responsibility for your actions. Even if you feel like you didn't do anything to deserve the treatment your received that much maybe true but there is three sides to every situation his side your side and the naked truth sometimes we don't embrace the truth sometimes it hurts but you must face it so you can move on into your destiny in God. Face it take responsibility and start your journey to emotional wholeness. Stay tuned there is more surprises to come.........

Chapter 5: THE BREAKING AWAY

In April of 2006 the man of my dreams made me his assistant pastor. Wow I was so positive that we would be married after this, after all he had shared the most important part of himself with me his ministry. I was so proud to become the assistant pastor officially. To tell the truth I had been functioning as the assistant from day one so to officially become the assistant pastor was just wonderful. Little did I know it was another set up to give me more responsibilities and to free the pastor up from some of the day to day operations of the ministry. Instead of us growing closer we started to grow apart. Because of his notoriety he was beginning to gain more popularity among the ladies in which they were giving him more attention. I told you in a previous chapter that women like men in authority. It's dangerous for a man who is not secure in himself to gain a lot attention that he is not use to getting it will cause them 1st to be distracted, and a false sense of pride. Things began to change and we began to spend less personal time together. One flaw that I saw in my knight in shining armor was that he was easily moved and influenced by person that seem to have authority. So people began to whisper in his ear. I feel he came to a point where he felt he didn't need me as much or that he could find someone better than me to be his companion. Through all of this I still remained faithful to the ministry. After all he had shared with his friend that I was the one so I didn't have to worry about him being with anyone else. Wow how wrong was I. Because he was so easily influenced by others by the way that is so dangerous for a pastor to so vulnerable yes it's good to hear others opinion but you must trust the voice of God.

By the end of 2007 I was fed up I told him repeatedly that we needed to talk but to no avail. During this time a sister at the church needed a place to live. She and her daughter moved in with me a major mistake. The enemy can use people to hinder you. Here it is I thought that I was helping a sister and she and her daughter betrayed my by taking things I would say out of context back to the pastor. So this caused a strain on our relationship. So in March of 2008 he had met someone. A woman's intuition is Gods build in GPS for us. I already knew. We had attended a church out of town. I was sitting in my truck I saw this lady and I said to myself that's the kind of lady he wants. Sure enough the following weekend at our singles conference this sister shows up at the church. I knew what was up. A few Sundays went by and the pastor and I went out to dinner. It was at this time that he told me that God told him to marry this lady. So I gut punched him and stated that I was getting married too. (I had told a lie to cover my feelings) His bottom lip quivered in surprise. When I left that restaurant I was devastated all my hopes and dreams and what I had envisioned is now all gone. I really could not cry because I was in shock. I went to a dear friend of mine house and she came out to my car I began crying to her and trying to explain to her what just had happened to me. She was sympathetic to me and she did understand because she too had been involved in a dysfunctional relationship with a "preacher". The pain in my chest was intense I felt so hopeless and helpless. How would I recover from this devastation? I've never been married but I can imagine what it feels like for someone to walk out on you and divorce you. I felt like something/ someone was ripped from my soul. It actually felt like someone had died. I went home that night and went to bed. I didn't sleep I lay there my mind racing what did I do wrong; I'm I not good enough for him? I felt alone and betrayed. I felt like everyone was laughing at me. I felt like a fool. I felt like God played a trick on me, because this was not what I had signed up for. I thought that this was the man of my dreams, my soul mate. I said to myself this must be a mistake. I didn't get any sleep that night but I did manage to get up out of bed and go to work. I had to put on a front for my consumers and for my employees. I worked hard that day to fight back the tears. I went to my mother's house after work. I lived with her during the week because my job was in my home town. I actually work for my sister as the Director of operations for a residential facility for children with mental challenges. I spent most of the first day after work in my room. How many know that a mother knows her child no matter how old the child maybe.

BACK TO LIFE

My mother made her way into the room where I lay. She says I know that there is something going on with you what is It.? I began to tell her and she was sympathetic with me. There is nothing like the comfort of a mothers words reassuring her child that it's alright and letting you know that you can make it. It was at that point that I decided to just take one day at a time.

He the x-man of my dreams attempted to call me but I refused to answer. Then he began to text me messages that assured me that he was concerned for me and that he was praying for me. Wow. As time progressed the next week on a Monday I decided to set a time to talk to him. We met in a mutual place and sat down to talk. I began to explain to him how I felt about him and that I just needed a break away from the church to collect myself. Because prior to our meeting I received a call from a Woman of God who didn't know what was going on. She had called to set up a ministry appointment for my pastor and wanted to know who was the secretary with the same last name as the pastor, and had he gotten married. I explained to her that the secretary was his sister-n-law. I did explain to her that he had just told me that he was getting married. She of coursed asked was it me I told her no. She was concerned about my well being. She advised me to make sure that my spirit was right before I did anything else at the church. She told me that the woman that is closes to the pastor help set the tone for the house. I knew that and I would never do anything to upset the flow of the anointing in the house of God. So I met with him to let him know that I just needed a break to get myself together he stated that he understood. At this point I had not planned on leaving the ministry after all I had worked just as hard if not harder than him in this endeavor. He asked me a question; he said how do you feel about me. I told him this, "If you love someone and love them right you will never stop loving them."

I was attempting to get myself together. Some members were concerned others nosy. I had begun getting calls from the ones that were concerned. I assured them that I was ok just taking a break and that I would be returning to in the next few weeks or so. Next thing I hear the pastor had a meeting with the church. He told them that I had abandoned my post and that I owed them an apology. He also shared with the congregation that I loved him so much and that I could not take the fact that he was getting married. WOW. I was crushed even more because he had betrayed our friendship and my trust. As a co-laborer in the gospel he should have had a sense of loyalty to cover me. I in fact had covered for him on many occasions. On top of everything that I had faced I also felt the feeling of being betrayed. This was the beginning of my breaking away...................................

At this point I had been crushed. I was left feeling like I had no other choice except to leave the ministry. My character, my integrity had been attacked and mauled. I had been betrayed in the worst sense of the word. Two people stood up in the meeting and stated that it was not fair what was stated about me because I was not there to defend myself. That made me feel good that out of all my years of laboring in the gospel there someone had gained something from my life and knew that I was a woman of integrity.

After much prayer and soul searching I decided that it would be best that I leave the ministry. My character had been tarnished in the eyes of the members by their pastor. I no longer felt that I would be effective in that ministry. So in May of '08 I turned in my letter of resignation. I again underwent a lot of agony within and without. Within because I again felt that I had lost a child. I had helped birth out this ministry and now I had to leave it behind. I can identify with a mother that has had to give up her child for a closed adoption. The emptiness that I feel was agonizing. I felt agony without because of the mouths of church people. The whole church community in that town knew what happened to me. I felt so ashamed. For a long time I didn't go to the stores in that town. I would go to stores in the neighboring towns to avoid seeing my x-church members and other church people we had fellowshipped with.

Stay tuned I am now on the journey...

BACK TO LIFE

Chapter 6: THE JOURNEY

Often in life we do not count up the cost when we make decisions. When I joined the church I never imagined in a thousand years that things would turn out like they did, but I knew enough about God to know that he had a master plan. He always causes us to triumph in the mist of our trouble. So what appears to others as total defeat He, God will turn into total victory. It's a process to get to that point of knowing that God will bring you out alright.

While we are going through our test it is very important to decide early on that you will not stay stuck in the same rut. I have always known that I had a higher purpose to fulfill and that I wanted to fulfill it. My first steps on this journey called recovery were a simple prayer. My prayer was Lord please do not allow the root of bitterness to take root in my heart, soul or spirit. I was determined to forgive and not allow this incident to stunt my growth in God. I have witness many people in this life be full of bitterness. Bitterness is an ugly, ugly spirit that will suck the life out of its victims.

While in this phase of recovery can be tricky because your emotions can be a rollercoaster. Your must deal with the anger, the grief, the feelings of loneliness, abandonment, betrayal and feeling of low self-esteem. The way to work through all of these is the word of GOD, Prayer, Praise and worship, and a good support system. You must be able to talk to someone and not necessarily for advice but at times just a sounding board someone to listen. This was the real combination that worked for me. In a lot of situations we as women just need the comfort of real friends and family that will support you and listen to you.

I must be transparent and honest their where times that I couldn't read the word, pray or talk to my support system all I could do is praise and worship God. Someone my say how could you praise God when your world had just fell apart? My response would be how could I not. The scripture says in everything give thanks for this is this is the will of Christ Jesus concerning you. Praise and worship will take you above your situation and cause you to see the Lord and bring you into his presents. The word is true in his presences is the fullness of Joy and on his right hand is pleasures for evermore. (Psalms 16:11) God brought so much healing to me through praise and worship. In those times I realized that God is truly the source of my strength and the strength of my life. In those times my relationship with God has intensified. I can truly say that I Love Him more now than I loved him in years past. I know that this sounds like a cliché but trials do come to make us stronger, and what doesn't kill you can only make you stronger. So to all my sisters out there who my find yourself in this situation or a similar situation my word to you is that you can make it just take one second, one minute, one hour, one day, one year at a time. Take your time and allow God to heal you. God used people to minister to me. It's good to be validated by people you respect in ministry. It also helps for you to gain a greater sense of who you are and what your purpose really is. All of this can aide you on your journey to healing.

You will know that you are healed when you are able to talk to the person that hurt you without any feelings of animosity and no feelings of anger against that person. I was able to hold a conversation with mister x-man of my dreams. I told him that I forgive him for what he done. This was important to me because I was ready to move into the next phase of life and next phase of ministry. It's very important to close chapters of your past so you can start the next book in your life. The x-man never apologized for what he done to me. So I had to come to grips with that and be ok with that. That was another hurdle I was confused because I expected him to apologize being that he is a man of the clothe. I had to realize that at that point it wasn't about him but about my forgiveness. I had to let that go and let God deal with him. I'm not responsible for how he treats me but I am responsible as a woman of God how I treat him. One of my high points in on my road to recovery and healing was that I was able to attend his church. Upon entering into that sanctuary again I had a flood of

BACK TO LIFE

emotions, nervous, excited, wondering how I would be received, confident, assured, transparent just a flood of emotions. Once I entered the actual sanctuary I feel a sense of peace and accomplishment because what I thought I would never be able to do just 3 years prior to this I did it Gods way. My main objective for going was to show the love of God that and to let the pastor and congregation know that I had no animosity toward them what so ever. To my surprise the pastor was talking about reconciliation in the body of Christ. Wow Gods timing is impeccable. I had planned to go earlier in the year but God gave me a specific time to go. While trying to get to the church guess what I had a flat tire. That was a sho nuff sign that it was Gods will for me to go to the church. It was the church anniversary that was another a ha moment because God has a way of letting us celebrate our victories. Once I entered in and he recognized that it was me he got up off the organ and embraced me and asked if I would have words. I said of course I would be honored. Not only was I able to enter into that church but God had so orchestrated for me to have an opportunity to say words of encouragement and love. He and I had an opportunity to chat after the service. I told him that God was glorified that day and that our ministries would be blessed forever.

I praise God for the journey and road to my healing it had highs and low, bends and curves and mountains and valleys, rivers and oceans but it been worth it because there is life after the healing……………………….

BACK TO LIFE

Chapter 7: LIVING LIFE

Thank God there is life after devastation. It took me three years to recover from this devastation. It's important to surround yourself with positive people and people who are genuinely concerned. After I left that ministry in the spring of 08 it was the enemies desire to see me stay at home and never go back to church but how many know that when you have purpose and destiny on your life you can't settle for being a quitter. I sat home for about 2 weeks and went to a church in a neighboring town and the woman of God called me out and ministered to me and told me what had happened to me and that God was starting the healing process. I went there for a few months and then God shifted me to The Door of Hope Christian Church where the senior Pastor is Bishop Michael Blue. I received so much healing from the word of God. I remember one Sunday he ministered to me and said all of the nonsense will soon make sense. That word stuck with me until this day and I declare that I can truly say that at this point in my life all the nonsense make sense.

In the spring of 2011 I launched the ministry that God gave me, Safe Haven Ministries. This was God original plan. I had ran from being a pastor but God has a way of bringing you into the place He intended for you. Being a founder and senior pastor has been so fulfilling. In the hour when people are throwing in the towel God has raised me up to be a voice of hope and a beacon of light for many. I'm in a place of complete happiness. I can say that I don't regret anything that I've gone through because it has truly prepared me for this time in the kingdom. I know that God has called me to minister to those who are hurting and empower them to carry out their purpose in the earth.

God is a wise investor and He knows how to get the glory out of our lives. Much of what we go through in life has very little to do with us but about the people we have to minister to. You can make it through any obstacle that the enemy puts in your way. With determination and a true love for God He will see you through it.

The spirit of manipulation isn't strong enough to stop destiny. Destiny is stronger than death even the death of a relationship. Once you are free from unforgiveness the possibilities and opportunities for your life are endless. I've suffered many things manipulation, rejection, dysfunction, abuse, etc but none were able to stop me. When God has a plan for your life if you stay with Him through it all you have no other choice but to make it.

To that sister or brother that has been hurt I'm a living testimony to let you know that there is life, purpose and destiny awaiting you on the other side of hurt.

The thief cometh not but for to steal kill and destroy, But I have come that you might have LIFE and that more ABUNDANTLY. (John 10:10).

Closing Prayer for the reader: Dear heavenly Father in Jesus name first I want to thank you for my life and the purpose you have given me.

Father in Jesus name I renounce and release any unforgiveness I maybe harboring in my heart. Father it's my desire to please you and I want to be completely free to operate in an authentic and genuine anointing in the kingdom. Lord perfect your love in me so that I can fully love and embrace those that have hurt me and minister to those that have incurred pain and hurt. I refuse to stay stuck. In Jesus name I'm moving forward. I press toward the mark of high calling in Christ Jesus my lord. I humbly ask you and I believe that it's done in Jesus Name. AMEN.

I AM LIVING LIFE AND SO CAN YOU.......

Moving forward..................

Stay

tuned..

BACK TO LIFE

About the Author

STEPHANIE Y. GENWRIGHT

Stephanie y. Genwright is a native of rural North
Carolina. She is a daughter, sister, aunt, niece and friend.
Stephanie has been a minister of the gospel of Jesus
Christ since the tender age of 16. In 2011 she was
promoted in the kingdom of God and began Pastoring.
She currently oversees several ministries. Her passion for
God and ministry has made her a well sought after
preacher in all type of venues. She has been featured in a
well-known gospel magazine Majesty Now.
Stephanie also works in the field of nursing as a Licensed
Practical Nurse. Her career has spanned over the course
of several decades.

Stephanie has dedicated her life to helping people whether through the vehicle of nursing or ministry. She believes that God is a holistic God and we should carry that same attribute. We must be concerned about the whole man to help make this world a better place.

BACK TO LIFE

Booking Request

To book the author please email **sgenwright@aol.com**
Facebook: Stephanie Genwright,
 Instagram: @stephaniegenwright
 910-918-7357 or Desheka James 843-610-1545

Pure Thoughts Publishing, LLC